Pieces of Me

-Nikki Farris

I want to take a moment to thank so many people who made this book possible.

To my family and friends who have stood by me through so much. Thank you for always being an unwavering support in my life. I hope you can understand all the love it took to make me feel so deeply at my core. That depth is what created this book. You nurtured that part of me, and for that I am forever thankful. Understand that every poem is a part of me and was written with the vulnerability and honesty most would reserve for their diaries. I write with raw emotion, in the moment so it is my sincerest hope that I never offend the ones I love.

To everyone who inspired me: Thank you. From the bottom of my heart, for the good, the bad, the ugly and the beautiful. I wouldn't be who I am today if not for every experience that sculpted me. The pain pushed me, the love supported me, and the conflict created me. Remember even the insignificant F*ck Boy can inspire.

To those who read my poetry and encouraged me; thank you for the push I needed. I am forever grateful for the support. I hope you weren't just being nice.

Some content may be triggering for those who have experienced physical, emotional or sexual abuse.

National Sexual Assault Hotline: 1-800-656-4673

National Suicide Prevention Lifeline: 1-800-273-8255

Writing is a wonderful outlet, but counseling, therapy and assistance are all part of recovery.

## *"Pieces of me"*

I'd give you my heart, but I left it between the sheets of a man I thought I loved until I tried.

You can't cry on my shoulder, for its still being leaned on in the aftermath of an old friend's devastation.

I gave my ears, without hesitation. I simply forgot to whom.

Spun my spine into a broken woman, till she could walk again.

I'm certain you'll find my liver in the bathroom of Jesse's old apartment beside my dignity.

My trust, weaved into the carpet of a dim hallway on Andrew Street.

My knees where they found the ground in the family room, at Claxton Hepburn Medical.

My innocence in my childhood bedroom.

I left my integrity at the door of a trap house.

Vulnerability laying on a couch.

My empathy in every room I comforted a person, while they felt for the exact vertebrae to put the knife in.

I've left pieces of myself with people who didn't deserve my time.

Vital organs, forgotten on bedside tables like lip-gloss left behind in the early morning afterglow.

Appendages strewn about like discarded clothes leaving a trail that is my life.

I'll lend you my eyes, and maybe, you'll see. Why I can't bear to go find them.

-NF

### *"Can You Answer Him?"*

1st Question

He asked

Does the blood freeze in your vein?

Too cold to reach each extremity?

Ice Princess

2nd question

Who broke you?

Or is the better question who didn't?

How many hands did it take to cause these cracks in your soul?

Can it be fixed?

3rd Question

I see you

Purse your lips as finger tips

Trace the scars of invisible wounds.

Does it scare you?

-NF

## *"My Life"*

I'm 8

I'm the butt of my father's jokes.

And everyone thinks it's funny

We pick on the people we love


I'm 10

Everyone leaves me

A 4 mile bike ride by myself

Kids are mean


I'm 15

After 4 years of sleepovers and secrets

My entire group of friends turn their backs on me

Adolescences is painful


I'm 22

My father is dead

My life is no longer a party

I'm no longer relevant

Adult friendships are difficult

I'm 29

And I'm out of excuses

For shitty people

-NF

### *"Keep Hating"*

Your blood boils as they sit and praise me

I see you size me up

Just know you can't take me

Withstood gale force winds

Your breeze can't break me

You can't faze me

This skin does bruise

These bones will break

But there's no limit

To the blows I'll take

-NF

### *"Car Stereo"*

The car stereo is a constant source of contention between us

I like hip hop, you like classic rock, there's no middle ground.

The only artist on which we agree is Tupac.

And even he has not produced enough music to fill the time we spend in my Monte Carlo.

Your insistence on controlling the radio has become a sore subject.

More than once you've changed my favorite song mid-verse

And even worse, you caught me singing out loud.

Thursday your Lynard Skynard CD got jammed in the deck

For days there has been peace in the front seat.

My new stereo gets installed on Tuesday.

-NF

### *"I Couldn't Help You"*

We were two broken people trying to fix each other.

Wrapping war wounds with good intentions that turned out to be tainted by the arsenic of our lifetimes.

Offering soothing words that seemed laced with disappointment

Your memories mirrored my memories.

Your experiences stirred my experiences.

Every shared story was like packing salt in a wound.

Every step in the right direction felt like walking on a broken leg too soon.

It took too long to realize I couldn't breathe life into you when I had but one breath left for myself.

-NF

### *"I'm Not Alone"*

I live with this hollow in my chest.

I sleep but I don't rest.

Some days with the morning light the pain will come.

Other days I wake comfortably numb.

I'll bear this burden on broader shoulders and refuse to sink.

But bear with me because some days it hurts to think.

I won't ask to please forget.

And I won't question why, so just let me sit.

I feel the pain ebb and flow.

I'm not holding on, but it won't let go.

I never asked for your sympathy.

Just sit with me.

Share some oxytocin bliss with me.

Someday this will all be history.

But for now

All I need

Is you to sit with me.

-NF

## *"Kelly"*

My idol

My sister

My other half

My sharer of pain

My secret sentinel

My echoed laugh

With all the love I have in my heart

I love you as if we are together, even when we're apart.

-NF

### *"Told You Too Much"*

I mapped out the grid to my heart

Showed you the seams from which you could rip it apart

Highlighted weak points

Planned the enemies attack

I was my own Benedict Arnold

Showed you everything I lack.

You asked for insecurities and weaknesses

Are you damaged goods?

My pen hesitated over paper.

As it knew it should

Against better judgment I prepared myself as a sacrificial offer

It reads

No weapon formed against me shall prosper

But what if I provided the ammo

And I loaded the gun?

For it was only due to Trojan arrogance

That the Spartans ever won.

-NF

### *"I wrote a poem"*

I wrote a poem

For you

Not for you

But about you

That statement seems more true

Because you'll never read it

And either will anyone else

Because then the world would see

How you got under my skin

But I read it

Again, and again

Sometimes out loud

Other times in my head

Two poems

It's actually two poems

I wrote for you, about you

With you in mind

If only you could see

How you inspired me

Left me aching for more

Three poems

I suppose this makes it three poems

-NF

### *"I Became Your Masterpiece"*

You taught me to paint a picture of perfection

Using broad strokes to obscure half truths

Dark colors to dissuade deep inquiries

Monet like motion to prevent prying eyes from ever focusing steadily on any one detail

Keep the outside world in a state of constant confusion

Idealizing the prowess, I choose to put on display

Never thinking to look for underlying meaning

Yes, a fine prodigy I made in the art of deception.

-NF

### *"All cried out"*

I don't hard cry anymore

You know that overwhelming emotional break

Here come the tears

Face distorted

Whole body shaking

Take ten minutes to compose yourself crying

I just don't have it in my anymore

-NF

### *"This one is not about you"*

I'm stuck in my head and I don't wanna be here right now

Questioning your intentions

Watching my resolve dissolve

Wishing I never listened to the lies coming out of your lips

Asking myself why I crossed that bridge for this emotional trip

Wondering is a wicked wind on which I easily get swept away

Patience: a virtue with which I was never instilled

Doubt a second nature heavily drilled into my head

You're not here but I still feel the warmth of your body beside me in my bed

Asking myself if I've affected you the way you've affected me

Now that I've shattered the illusion and allowed you to see

Just below the surface

And was it worth it?

Years of pining for a female that could never be the epitome of perfection you once thought she was

The personification of an angel you once saw sleeping on a couch

Within arm's reach, but you couldn't reach out and touch her

With all the bravery you could muster

Bared your soul, told her you loved her

For her to put up a wall

And years later to let that façade fall

And now I wonder

Why did I bother?

Knowing I could never live up to the expectation.

-NF

### *"You want the truth?"*

Truth is; you don't know me

Took one look, tried to pigeonhole me

It's a matter of fact you can't control me

Fuck with me, Imma leave you lonely

Wanna play games, you better learn to live without me

Move so smooth, you should never doubt me

I'll give my all when it's right

Break my back day and night

But Ill flip that switch no hesitation

Bounce out this bitch no reservations

Soft as silk, but cold as ice

Not just once, I told you twice

Thought you heard, guess you don't listen

Too distracted by trifles that glisten

I kept it real; you tried to play it cool

Peep this gesture, 'cause you're the fool.
-NF

### *"Forgotten"*

I feel like I was forgotten the moment I was born

Do you think a nurse chased my parents down to place me in their arms before they hit the exit?

At 4 my mother forgot to get me off the head start bus more times than she'd like to admit

Do you know how many times you need to be left at the grocery store before you learn to keep a close eye on the adult who's supposed to keep a close eye on you?

Two

Two times

Can you decipher the look on an adult's face when you walk in and your parents are gone?

Their mouth says, "They'll be right back" but the arch of their eyebrow says as soon as I tell them you're still here

After school activities are a gamble

You'll lose

Using payphones to call home because they didn't show

My father left me

At malls

Garages

Jobsites

Friends' houses

And once at Can-Am

I've sat on too many curbs wondering if they're wondering where I am

Do you know how it feels to be forgotten?

-NF

### *"You were never the one"*

Some days I wish I never met you

And I wish you felt the same

It's been years since you crossed my mind

I no longer covet your name

See I idolized our image, not our reality

Because in reality

You made empty promises with hollow words

Missed birthdays

And sent presents that told my heart

This is all you deserve

You bought complacency with currency

Feigned empathy when you felt urgency

And at times I believe even you thought you had fallen in love

But I know

You know

That's not what we were made of

I'm mad at the girl who thought she loved you

And the man that let her believe

I'm mad at the girl who let you stay

And the man who knew he should leave

-NF

### *"Black notebooks and little red albums"*

I take pictures of myself from various angles because one day I won't look like this anymore

I support the movement to embrace inner beauty, but I also like the way I look right now

Especially in a $50 bra from an overhead left angle, good lighting and my hair tossed over my shoulder

And while I may maintain my sarcasm and wit, I won't look like this when imp older

I do this strictly for self-esteem preservation

Now I'm not saying, on occasion, during late night texting conversation

I won't share one for purely instant gratification, but that's not my main motivation.

See I save them, and I print them, and I put them in my little red album

Which is tucked discreetly in my closet behind more clothes than I could fathom

Because someday when the face looking back at me isn't quite tight anymore, and my eyes have lost some of their shine

I can pull out that little red album and say, 'damn I used to be fine.'

-NF

### *"Charlie"*

You're an experience

All blue eye and sincere smile

"hey"

Words lost on my lips

DJ booth in the living room

Lead me up the stairs

Every encounter has its own playlist

Stage lights glistening across the walls

Intimate introductions followed by fierce hands

Find myself in a trance between the sheets

And then you dance me to the door

"Call me"

-NF

### *"I forgot to save him"*

I told him "I will save you."

But life kept getting in the way

I remember sitting on the edge of the tub in the basement bathroom

As far from them as we could get

Battle brewed above us

He told me "I hate them."

And I promised I would save him

Who would have thought?

Here I would sit

Haunted

By late night pacts

Made with tear filled eyes

I forget when I stopped hiding in corners and began moving in the dark

When I stopped sheltering him from neglect and we started using it to our advantage

When did we forget we wanted more?

And instead became everything we hated

I promised I would save him

I failed

I lied

I never even tried

-NF

### *"I ache for you"*

I want to feel my fingertips trace the curve of your face

Brush my lips across your widow's peak

Feel the warmth of your cheek against my cheek

Because I ache for you

I still recall the weight of your head on my shoulder

Re-imagine it now with you older

Your palms pressed against mine

Gentle fingers intertwine

There's a pit in my stomach

A hole in my heart

It's a pain that's so deep, it tears me apart

I still ache for you.

-NF

## *"Her"*

She's got a tough exterior

A face formed of laugh lines and furrowed brows

Very few have seen her with wide wet eyes

She doesn't bear the trails of tear stained cheeks

Someone taught her to catch teardrops on fingertips before they could ruin her makeup

She's made up of generations of tough women

Years of 'don't cry's,' and 'be strong's'

She doesn't need someone to hold her together

She needs someone to let her fall apart.

-NF

### ***"Dad"***

You come to me in my dreams

They're simple moments

You're sitting in your chair

That smile on your face

Asking how I got so ugly

And in those moments

It's as if you never left me

-NF

### *"You'll learn"*

You feign emotion

To get what you desire

I try to feign interest

But quickly I tire

At one point

Games had been my specialty

But I grew up

And you will too

Eventually

All I ask

Is you come correct with me

If not

I suggest

You watch your step with me

Cold as ice I'll remain

But ill match pain for pain

Especially

When you disrespecting me

I admit

When I was young

I was a bitch

Collectively

You twisting trust for vengeance

That's straight treachery

You could have had the best of me

Instead

You'll learn

Not to mess with me

-NF

### *"Just Tell 'em"*

Yours is a story that's not easy to tell

See it's not always where you land, but how far you fell

Not how far you rise

But how hard you fight

Not how many tries it takes

Just that you tried until you made it right

When they haven't faced your options, they won't understand your choice

So, make them hear the passion in your words

Feel the pain in your voice

Bear your truth

It's inspiring

Even though

It's tiring

And uphill battles will not cease

You'll still rise

Until you find your peace

-NF

### *"A mother's heart"*

The human heart beats 100 times per minute

Pumps five liters of blood per minute

It is the strongest muscle in the human body

Never resting from birth to death

Mothers are the strongest member of any family

Withstanding childbirth and teenage hate

Capable of lifting a car to save a child

Willing to sacrifice dreams, aspirations, dignity and life itself to provide and protect their offspring

A mother's heart

The strongest muscle residing in the strongest member of your family

And I broke it

I broke my mother's heart

She found the pieces

Put them back in their places

Moved forward with this challenge she faces

But I see the cracks

Hear the catch in her voice

Feel the pain between the lines of the things she says and those she leaves unsaid

I broke my mother's heart

And she never forgave me

Because she never blamed me

But I can't stop blaming myself

-NF

### *"Charred"*

I've felt granite hands on porcelain skin

Till porcelain turned to marble and the only pain came from within

How you couldn't tell I was broken

I'll never understand

While I may have put me back together

I did so with a shaky hand

If you look closely you can see

These cracks run deep

It's staying strong for now

But this hold won't keep

I took venomous verbal lashings

They burned from within

Charred the depths of my soul

To the darkest of sin

-NF

### *"Damaged Petals"*

I wasn't raised I grew

Unlike you

I wasn't carefully tended and pruned to be a prize-winning rose

I was untamed and untended like a wild weed grows

I took what I needed; survival is all that I know

And I thrived in destruction, that's how wildlife goes

Damaged leaves in the process and some petals have tares

But I dragged myself through the wreckage and every piece was still there

May not be award worthy

With a prized garden plot

But I fought and I struggled

For everything that I got.

-NF

## *"Nice Try"*

When you found me

I was perpetually damaged

You failed to see the fine lines and cracks that covered every inch of me

But I saw the look in your eyes

You thought you could break me

If 27 years couldn't destroy me

I sure wouldn't falter for you

-NF

### *"She was a wild woman"*

She lived life by a philosophy she found in red graffiti

On the streets of New York City

She danced to her own beat in the rain

With mud on her face

Keeping pace, to the wind

She sought solace in sunsets she believed were sculpted just for her

And she fought fear with laughter

Even after

She felt the deepest of pains

She waged wars with demons

And in between them

She conquered her own corner of hell

She was a wild woman

With fire in her soul

She roared like the ocean

Beautiful and out of control

-NF

### *"On a cold winter night"*

Red lights in the rearview

"Sir I need you to exit the vehicle."

This is not a routine traffic stop

I'm 13

He's 11

In a matter of moments my life shattered

We're riding home in the back of a cop car

I want to tell him everything's alright

But I won't lie to him

Standing in the front yard of our family house like this life belongs to someone else

Let in like strangers in our home

They're sitting on the antique red velvet couch we don't sit on

She's handcuffed in front

He's handcuffed in back

He's thirsty

My brother offers his soda

It's Barqs

He prefers IBC

But he's thirsty

Suddenly I'm aware of the soda in my own hand, but I don't move

The officer won't let my brother cross an invisible line on floor

Have you ever seen a handcuffed woman help a handcuffed man drink?

They handle it like professionals

"Time to go Steve."

They rise slowly from the couch

Invisible lines reinforced by human shields

"We'll be there before the sunrises."

Even handcuffed he's 77" of swagger

This time my father didn't forget me.

-NF

### *"I'm Tired"*

I'm tired of biting my tongue till it's numb

Staying silent because nice things never come

I'm tired of hood credit and street games

Of entitled females I'd rather call by lesser names

Thinking they slick with they shit talking ways

Giving themselves accolades they don't even earn these days

I'm tired of hearing saved stories

Fake glories

My ears bleed from the onslaught of demolished English language

Twisted to tell stories no one cares about

False tales to hide hard times

I'm tired

Of people taking reservation and respect

As a sign of bowing down

Politeness for passivity

Of pasting a smile on my face

As I taste

Bile creep up my throat

I'm tired

-NF

### *"You Can't Understand"*

It fed the darkest part of me

Dripped

From fingertips

From the first touch

 So slick

Like oil spreads

Too quick to question

Too dark to mention

How could I describe?

Even if I found the words, you'd think I lied

From the first touch it consumed me

I shuddered

But not a single objection was muttered

Contrary

I begged for more

Let skin deep dive

Till it altered my core

-NF

## *"I suppose it's possible"*

You expect me to accept that the ability to nurture just wasn't in your nature?

Could it be my fault for idolizing the effects of affection and the capacity of heartwarming moments?

Perhaps parenting was not part of your programming

I apologize for always asking for something you simply could not give

If I could have foreseen the rift my expectations would create perhaps, I would have settled for what you were capable of giving.

-NF

### *"Dear John"*

When I fell in love with you there were things about you, I could not see

Now that it's over let them know it was you it was not me

I finally realized I could no longer exchange bruises for roses

Your sorrow filled tender kisses could no longer heal broken noses

There was never enough makeup to cover all your hate

Never enough words to remove you from that violent mental state

Just like you, all your promises were broken

Your apologies, as manipulative as the lips from which they were spoken.

-NF

### *"That's Why"*

I was loyal to the game

It was never loyal to me

Pulled knives outta my back

Every day

That's how it be

Paid bills in houses that didn't have my name

Filled fridges that fed others, filled me just the same

Paid for birthdays and Christmases for kids I didn't bear

I was the one you called when no one else was there

I sat back, took note, you thought I didn't listen

I heard every word; there wasn't shit that I was missing

When I was up, y'all was all around

Hit bottom looked up, realized y'all was never down

-NF

### *"Have you ever"*

Certain fabrics make my skin crawl with the memory of close-knit carpet against my face.

Blood mixed with bile in the back of your throat, do you know the taste?

Know how rug burn on sunburn stings?

Felt flashbacks that only pulled tight drawstrings can bring?

It goes black

When you look back

And you don't know if it was all in your head or the whole world heard your screams

Frantically pulled on stockings

Skintight and ripped right at the seams

With no energy left to exert but you walked with the sheer power of will

Dressed for a summer's heat but shivering in a cold world's chill

Pressed on with forced steps to the doorstep of a friend who won't pry

Found the voice you thought you left in that dark hallway and said, just don't cry.

Exhaled

Knocked

And prayed

Lord don't let these flood gates break

So just know that

I know that

I'm the type men would take

-NF

### *"Tyga"*

I dreamt that we were curled together

You were in my arms

A smile on your face

Sleeping like we always used to

A brief yet vivid memory

And then I woke

Tears filled my eyes

Sometimes pain is beautiful

-NF

### *"Hidden"*

She hid them

Like a forbidden lover

Between the covers

Of books already written

She quickly became smitten

With the smell of published pages around her creation

A sensation

She felt she could only imitate

By letting her lines penetrate

Another's tome

She feared her words would never be worthy

Of a home of their own

-NF

### *"Thank you"*

Praise makes me tense

I'm much better at secondhand compliments

I'm rather familiar with the English language

Yet certain phrases

Elude my daily vocabulary

"I'm proud of you."

This simple declaration left me

Too stunned to speak

Too stuck to think

I don't know the proper decorum

For a concept, so foreign

Thank you doesn't seem capable of conveying the emotions those words stirred

Yet

It was all my lips could manage

-NF

### *"Five Years"*

I stopped hating you

When you stopped hitting her

And I stopped hating her

When she stopped blaming us for you beating her

And for five years I got to love you like a daughter should

Five years more than I ever thought I would

-NF

### *"This Christmas"*

Can you just breathe with me?

Let's take a moment

Set aside Christmas lists and great distances

And just breathe with me

Forget the pain of failing to make one day perfect

Let go of the expectation of Christmas morning

Instead

Let's focus on the other 364 days

The love that you give

The example of strength that you live

The daily inspiration

That you embody

Let's focus

On the 364 days

You spent

Bettering yourself

And humbly

Providing service

This Christmas

Let's take a moment

See the blessing that is this life

And that you are to others

And know

No gift

Nor meal

Can ever

Compare

To what you have given of yourself

Breath with me

-NF

### *"The Petty"*

The petty is real

So real

It's practically published

Embossed

Leather bound

Helvetica typeset

On weighted cream paper

The petty is deep

It resides at the center of my soul

It's a core part of me

Runs through me like a main artery

A straight pipeline to the aorta

It intertwines

With every vertebrae of my spine

A spinal tap reveals

85% petty

It remains in the oldest part of my brain

Releasing with a surge of serotonin

Oh, the petty is real

-NF

## *"Forgive me"*

I let you spend nights alone when I should have been there

Had words to comfort you but instead left you with dead air

Recognize the hurt in your eyes but no one taught me to comfort your pain

You think I'm cold and I'm distant let me explain

No one held my hand on bad days or tucked me into bed

I never got bear hugs or soft kisses on my head

No one wiped away my tears and told me it would be alright

Never had protection from things that went bump in the night

Learned to be strong because no one let me be weak

Kept my feelings to myself because no one asked me to speak

So, I may not know the right words, or use the right tone

But as long as I'm here, know you won't be alone

-NF

***"BFF"***

You're the strongest person I've ever known

The only person I can lean on and stand as tall as I do on my own

I never asked you to share this burden

But still you were there when I couldn't bear the pain

I would stand by you through the fire

Because you stood by me in the rain

-NF

## *"Why were you so weak?"*

You were born demanding

Raised fighting

Slapped down

You stood up

Broken

Put yourself back together

Pirouetted with pain

Danced with danger

You dabbled with destruction out of boredom and walked away unscathed

But not this time

This time

You crawled into the hellfire

Burrowed yourself into a demon's lap

Felt the flames flicker across bare skin

You sought the comfort of sin

Felt the pain of inevitable damage

But couldn't find the strength to crawl out of its grasp

Why were you so weak?

-NF

### *"Don't quit on me"*

I failed you

I shattered the image of your little girl

The one you held so dear

My shoulders slumped

Gaze averted

Can't look in the mirror

I know you're disappointed

You're angry

You just want me to get it right

More than ever I need you

So, rally

Don't give up the fight

Please

Don't quit on me

-NF

## *"No Participation Trophy Needed"*

Champions learn endurance

Athletes endure training

Quarterbacks endure tackles

Runners endure distance

Snowboarders endure cold

Boxers endure blows

I've endured

Busted knuckles

Black eyes

Dislocated knees

Broken hearts

And betrayed loyalties

I am a champion of pain

-NF

### *"You Can Need Me"*

Some people will need you more than you'll ever need them

They may need to put their knees in your back

Their feet on your shoulders

Their nails in your skin

To pull themselves back up

But isn't your back strong

Can't your shoulders bear the weight?

Don't you stand as tall today as you did before they climbed up your spine?

Using each vertebra like a ladder rung

Sure, those bruises hurt

Those claw marks stung

But can't you withstand the pain

Can't you be the 65" lift in someone's life?

Rest better at night knowing some people will need you more than you'll ever need them

-NF

## *"Notebooks"*

I like dollar store notebooks

There's no pressure

Their pages don't judge

Their lines are fine with my chicken scratch

Half sentences

Unfinished stanzas

Climbing up the page at 45-degree angles

These cardboard covers don't judge content

All words are worthy

Wide ruled allows room for correcting errors

Hard covers and pretty pages are intimidating

Takes time to build up the courage to taint the page of anything above a five star

The nicer the notebook, the longer the hesitation

I was gifted a handcrafted artisan notebook 8 years ago

The pages are still blank

-NF

### *"I Just Didn't Have the Words"*

I couldn't find a way to tell you

Sifted through every word that I knew

Tried out every combination

But none of them would do

Practiced speeches

Apologies

Went through a dozen revisions

But even Webster's dictionary

Couldn't explain this decision

So, I formulated the sentences

Again, and again in my head

But they were never quite right

So, they all went unsaid

As I sit enveloped in hesitation

At the coming of the dawn

I realize time for explanation

Has come and has gone

-NF

### *"Will I Ever Be the One?"*

I've got housewife hobbies

With street life history

I've got sea deep secrets

Where you're looking for an air of mystery

You might miss me when I'm gone

The loss of the laughter

Might leave you yearning for sarcasm and witty repertoire

And punchlines of self deprecation

You might hunger for my four course meals

Sprung out of half course kitchens

Mixed with unbelievable tales of misspent youth

You may lust for me

For secrets that lay behind sly smiles

For favors

And behaviors

We don't talk about in mixed company

You'll find comfort in me

Like that old Carhartt hoodie

Warn soft by your hard edges

Your favorite leather chair

Always there

When you need to relax

But you'll never love me

-NF

### *"Even if I told you"*

There's time I lost

But I can justify the cost

But the pain

I can't explain

With words I can't share

Because you

Weren't there

You can't understand the weight of a hand

When the love of a man

No longer outweighs the hate in his heart

You know when it all fell apart?

When expectation met reality

They could no longer live in duality
but it was so nice living in a fantasy

See we never planned to be

Such a volatile combination

Destroying hope without hesitation

It took every part of me

To walk away and still have a part of me

See I'm not the same woman I once was

You don't get it

It's ok

No one does

-NF

### *"The Reason I Write"*

Sometimes you have to write from places you no longer reside

Expose memories you built fortresses to hide

There's only so long you can let thoughts bounce around in your mind

When you put pen to paper you know what we find

Confessions

Obsessions

Internal tensions

The shit so dark you never mention

How you gonna get it off your chest?

Put pen to paper

It'll feel safer

Let your hand do the rest

-NF

### *"My Fault"*

You needed words, but I couldn't speak

Lost my voice let out a silent shriek

History made a Valkyrie meek

Wicked ways turned a wise woman weak

So, I pour my heart in 16 bars

Pull this hoodie tight to cover pristine scars

Bear my soul in onyx ink

Tear up the page 'cause loose lips sink

Haunted by memories to dark to share

Tried to explain but the words weren't there

It's not your fault it was never fair

I always showed up, but I was never there

Took too long to realize

Your heart couldn't heal their lies

What's dead never dies

You fell in love with empty eyes

-NF

### *"It's Not That Serious"*

I'm nobody's keeper

I don't wish to be kept

While you were out scheming

I peacefully slept

I desire devotion

I simply haven't found yet

So, until it's discovered

Your just another I've met

Forgive any misleading

For it's not what I meant

I'm simply nobody's keeper

And I don't wish to be kept

-NF

## *"Untitled"*

I felt this weight on my shoulders

It slid into my chest

I felt it burrow deeper

Turning a nagging feeling into a state of unrest

Felt it brew in the heart of me

Until it gnawed at a part of me

It grew something dark in me

At first it felt foreign

But then I felt nothing at all

Callous can't begin to explain

How it feels when you lose all hope, regret, guilt

You feel no pain

The devil makes you feel indomitable

Talons sink and try to gain control

Yet something still stirred inside of me

Something fierce survived in me

A will so resistant even in pitch dark it thrived in me

It fought against the pythons hold

Bucked and thrashed

And at last

I shook the devil out of my soul

## *"Looking back"*

I never acknowledged your presence

Not once did I question

Why I continued to move forward

Managed to fight

On days I shouldn't have survived

How I made it through the night

When I fell I never asked

If it was you who extended a hand

Never thought to look

For your footprints in the sand

Never questioned how people came at my weakest

That seemed heaven sent

Or stopped to wonder how at my darkest

I found the strength to repent

It was you who allowed me to see beauty

In my ugliest form

Provided a guiding light

Through this never-ending storm

You were my company

When I kept the world at arm's length

Woke me up many mornings

When I didn't have the strength

When I was broken

You held together the pieces

When I was ready

Dusted me off

Ironed out the creases

And not once did you ask for an ounce of recognition

Gave support without a single condition

I now realize

After everything I've been through

I'm still standing

All because of you

-NF

## *"Where were you"*

You weren't there when I needed you the most

So, I found myself seeking comfort in your promises ghost

I felt the chill run down my spine as I sat there alone

Empty words couldn't warm me all on their own

Good intentions couldn't ease the panic in my chest

Between each shallow breath I believed in you less and less

-NF

### *"The Woman's War"*

A war wages within us

We battle the image before us

Ignore the traits others adore in us

Moisturize

Conceal

Line

Pluck

Paint

We dye

Fry

Sew in what won't grow in

Diet? Try it

Waist train

Perfection endures pain

A war wages between us

Female on female hate

Our mothers and their mothers

Stood together

To better

Our circumstance

And we tear each other apart

At every chance

Project our insecurities

Until they affect another

Words hurt?

Who needs words?

We've mastered non-verbal blows

We throw disdain with curled lips

As if it were elbows

And as their confidence staggers

We send daggers

With side-eye glances

What are our chances?

When we tear each other down

When we should be building each other up

I have sinned against my sister

Forgive me

Wage this war with me

Those that came before us

Stood against greater odds

In worse circumstance

Stand with me

So, our daughters' daughters

Can stand a chance

-NF

### *"Just Fyne"*

Something about him puts me at ease

Truth slips through my lips without hesitation

It seems more than a mild infatuation

But I can't tell

I know no intimacy, without physical intimacy

I've never felt a connection without first establishing a sexual history

This feeling is foreign, and it's got me fucked up

I'm ashamed to explain that when I bear my heart to this man, I feel no shame

I question how long I can keep this attention

Not that I doubt his intentions

But I feel my every nerve tensing at the slightest mention of something deeper than sexual tension

Here's my self-fulfilling prediction

That while he displays that truest conviction

I'll be caught in this current of past predilection

Still standing here wondering what it is that I'm missing

And while my mind screams for me to move toward him

There's part of me that will just keep listing

-NF

## *"Still Fyne"*

We went on a date once

It was epic

But we never sealed the deal

Our chemistry is college level intense

The physical attraction immense

But are intellectual conversations are priceless

From dusk till the crack of dawn

I fight exhaustion, stifle yawns

Just to converse

With the best man in the business to talk a girl to sleep

Because I would rather risk sleeping on the phone than hang up
before I have to

After so many late-night lectures and deep revelations

I can lie to myself, but he sees through me

Show the rest of the world what I want

But he sees me fully

While I can shrug off loss like an insignificant Mortal Kombat
round

I leveled with myself

Realized I'd found the one man that can break me

Sealing the deal would be like sealing the fate

Stamping an expiration date on our friendship

Because my relationships are terminal

He blames the caliber of man I invest in

Tells me I look for love in all the wrong places

Breaking my back to put smiles on all the wrong faces

Says I treat basic boys like royalty

Sculpting love out of lust instead of loyalty

But this is the love I choose

Because you can't miss something you weren't afraid to lose

-NF

***"Premonition"***

I fell in love with locked doors

With a story that's not yours

I could see deceit in your eyes

Willfully weaved myself into your lies

When webs caught, I pulled in closer

Heard your warning, but it was already over

Grew up knowing life hurts

Fuck fear go feet first

Saw the outcome before we began

Surrendered to the current, I'm fates biggest fan

If I could go back, I'd do it again

It's only by our losses we can measure a win.

-NF

### *"Why car rides are dangerous"*

I've had some of my favorite memories in front seats

And yours was no exception

That laugh Intoxicating

Smile perfection

My side's stitched

Cheeks ache

Chest hurts

Like foresight already feeling my heartbreak

But I'm stuck

No choice

That voice

Dances down my spine

Legs tense I plant my feet

Suddenly your 6ft tall

I've shrunk in my seat

I'm now fully aware

Of every ounce of charisma coursing through the air

Just another little cruelty

Because there's no future for you and me

But in this moment, it's all I can feel

You leaned back laughing

Hand on the wheel

Forever burned in my brain

Bittersweet

but beautiful Just the same

-NF

### *"Once Upon a Time"*

I'll tell you her story so forget what you heard

She grew in a world built of ugly words

Survival required a face void of emotion

Self-expression was an uncharted ocean

Blessed with a voice no one wanted to hear

Learned vulnerability was the only evil she should fear

So, she crafted castles of beautiful language she kept all to herself

Slayed insecurities and collected moments as wealth

She believed entireties are overrated but moments are gold

She watched relationships get tainted, but her memories never grew old

She breathed easier, draw bridges pulled high

And you sat there in judgment, but never asked why

-NF

### *"All the Bad Days"*

You brought out the Monday in my life

The stress and the strife

The unwanted expectation

Waking with that dreaded sensation

You entered my life and the Weekday anxiety crept in


I wish you could have been my Sunday

My relaxation

My rehabilitation

My well rested indulgence

Baggy T-shirt and sweat pant acceptance

My gourmet tastes

Served on paper plates


But you insisted on Friday night expectations

Eight-hour days followed by high heel obligations

You wanted contoured cheeks and drawn out eyes

Painted lips pursed to tell white lies

You wanted the me I could be

But it wasn't healthy

You yearned for a walking talking selfie

### *"Untitled"*

In a bed of thorns, I found my safety

Pain made me who I am, it'll never break me

Do I remember happiness? I tell 'em faintly.

Midnight is my hour, daylight escapes me.

-NF

### *"My Truth"*

I know I'm a lot

How? 'Cause somebody told me.

Said your too much to handle I can't stand your pace.

Nah, though. He said it so sweetly, his hand on my face.

Said, you're 24-7 I'll give you ten on the three.

And that was still more than he'd ever give me.

Sat back, here getting lied to

Friends don't understand, I don't even like you.

They say you deserve better; they say it so surely.

What they don't understand is I was broken so early

Seen every man that I loved treat women so greasy

When you've seen true human nature, it don't make it that easy

So, for all man kind I Set low expectations

Moved on all man time with no hesitation

Took what I wanted with no reservations

So, when you hear him say "Fuck This Bitch" No need to console me

See some women want love, but this this is the old me.

-NF

### *"After Our Third Date"*

Russ said, hurt people hurt people, and that's the truth

Explains the pain I felt throughout my youth

Hard to move forward when I'm still feeling so haunted

To know what love looks like when I'm used to feeling unwanted

You say you love my company

But I keep asking what you see in me

Have no faith in monogamy

Still I'll give you all my loyalty

Because here you came as if I spoke you into existence

So, I meet your affection with tethered resistance

Struggling against every internal insistence

Wanting to trust this feeling, but the past is persistent

I whispered

"He's too good to be true."

My words echoed back

"He's just too good for you."

I can't bear for you to see these lines and these cracks

So, your pulling me closer, but they're holding me back

I'm holding my breath

That's what broken people do

Come close

Because even though I'm broken, I won't break you too

-NF

### *"ILoveYou"*

Hear your heart racing

Feel mine skip

Thoughts threatening to form sentences

I bite my lip

Eight letters in succession

Without a single space

Lost in thought,

You brush your lips across my face

If I only I could stop for a minute

My Minds off on its own pace

Indulging this moment of sweetness

Dripping with ambrosias taste

Eight little letters

Lingering on my tongue

Tight lipped,

Head spun

Feel it in my heart

Know it in my head

Eight silent letters

Simply go unsaid

-NF

### *"And Counting"*

The love I've known

Was fickle and fleeting

Moves in on a Monday

Come Friday it's leaving

Left with a swiftness

Twice as quick as it came

Left behind the pictures

Packed up the frames

It's hard to change something

You know at your core

So between every I love you

I'm waiting for you to walk out that door

So I'm holding your hand

As if you could just slip away

Embracing every minute

As if it's part of our very last day

I told you I trust you

Believe me I tried

But for every man that I've trusted

A part of me died

So to you it's just Sunday

But if you ask me

It's the day you didn't leave

Number 363

-NF

## "US"

You are music

Fingers keeping the base line

Feet providing percussion

Every muscle moving to the melody


I am lyrics

My hips know the hook

I vibrate with the verses

Every word winds down my spine.


Be My Music

I'll be your message.

-NF

## "_We were never really friends_"

I was your anchor, your confidant, your partner in crime

I had your back, but did you ever have mine?

I forgave your trespasses, your indiscretions, because others did worse.

I fell back, took my distance. But you did it first.

I was your ride or die, I'm done riding for free.

You were down for whatever

Something better

Just never

For me.

See I was dying

Never asked for a dime

Now I'm thriving.

Why would I ask for your time?

-NF

### *"This one's dark."*

I write poems about rape

Molestation

About parts of myself being taken.

But you don't ask.


I know,

That you know

That I know you know

But we won't talk about it.


I wish true words could tumble

From my lips

Without eloquence

Just once.


Can I tell you how I was broken without allegory?

Can I not personify my pain? And just tell you it fucking hurts.


Because as I lay here wide awake

Tears trailing down my face

You drift asleep holding me tight.

I have to wonder

Am I still allowing myself to be nothing more than a comfort thing?

Am I comforting?

Am I just making myself smaller to fit into the crook of your arm?

Shrinking to be something lovable.


I don't feel important

But I never died

So why is it killing me now?

-NF

## *"One Morning"*

With Tears in my eyes I woke

Wrote the saddest words I ever wrote

Face Flushed

Out of bed I rushed

To find paper and pen

Before the pain was lost again

Where it came from, it wasn't mine.

But now that it's written it stays on my mind.

-NF

### *"Here I stand"*

Here I stand, wind whipped by vulnerability

Wanting for once to be true to me.

I burnt bridges that never should have been built.

Didn't like the way the world looked, so I put it on a tilt.

Tore down walls that for years served a purpose.

Gave you a glimpse, just below the surface.

Was it worth it?


Here I stand

Mask off.


Can I stand?

With this cast off?


It's something I've only dreamt of.

If only for this moment, I let me feel my love.

-NF

## *"Poetic Indifference"*

Sit

If you read this you won't feel it like you'll feel it if I read it to you.

My lines flow so smoothly, they form foreign languages like ancient voodoo

And I curse you

Your plight?
To listen to ugly things discussed in beautiful ways

See my lines form, stanzas and poems that go on for days.

Through my words you'll see every confrontation

See how every situation is made greater through public escalation

See every contemplation

Feel my every emption.

From pain to ecstasy and everything in between.

But it's nothing that you haven't seen

It's the way I wrap everything in delicate verse.

Leaving you not knowing what one is better or worse.

See I paint tragedy in beautiful circumstance.

Sketch lives full of happiness that never had a chance.

So sit.

If you read this you won't feel it like you'll feel it if I read it to you.

My lines flow so smoothly they form foreign languages like ancient voodoo.

And I curse you.

-NF

Made in the USA
Middletown, DE
13 March 2022

62501162R00061